THE POSTCARD HISTORY SERIES

Salisbury
MARYLAND

THE POSTCARD HISTORY SERIES

Salisbury

MARYLAND

John E. Jacob

ARCADIA

Published by Arcadia Publishing,
an imprint of Tempus Publishing, Inc.
2 Cumberland Street
Charleston, SC 29401

Printed in Great Britain.

Library of Congress Catalog Card Number: 98-87136

For all general information contact Arcadia Publishing at:
Telephone 843-853-2070
Fax 843-853-0044
E-Mail arcadia@charleston.net

For customer service and orders:
Toll-Free 1-888-313-BOOK

Visit us on the internet at http://www.arcadiaimages.com

CONTENTS

ACKNOWLEDGMENTS

I would like to thank all the members of the Delmarva Postcard Club for their support, but particularly Henrietta Moore for her invaluable help as a critic and proofreader of my text. I would also like to thank Jessica Anderson, Janet Carver, Dr. Laurence Claggett, James Jackson, and Eugene Wharton for sharing their collections with me. I would like to thank my wife, Diane, for her patience and forbearance with cards that were strewn about the house. I cannot say thanks enough to my former secretary, Retta Mills, for her terrific tolerance of my handwriting, her assiduous supervision of my text, and her long-suffering patience and aid in getting my work ready for the publisher. I would also like to thank Silvia Taylor, Ernest Culver, Ned Fowler, and Robert Cannon for access to their collections as well as that of the Wicomico County Free Library. Also I would like to say thank you to Mark Bowen, the clerk of court, and to Anne Clay, a title researcher, for their assistance in the record office.

INTRODUCTION

Salisbury's history is tied in with the division of Somerset County into two parts. One part, later Worcester County, had a town suitable to be its county seat, but Somerset did not. Ten years before the 1742 separation, John Caldwell put a bill in the legislature to create a town, naming himself and four other individuals as a commission to lay out the town. Salisbury was formed by an act of the provincial legislature in 1732. Caldwell's bill stirred the opposition of Levin Gale, a fellow member of the legislature, who put in a bill in 1733 to found Princess Anne. The prize they fought for was the location of the county seat once Somerset was divided into two counties, Somerset and Worcester, in 1742. (Princess Anne was eventually chosen over Salisbury, and the defeat was accentuated by the fact that the dividing line between the counties ran "over John Caldwell's mill dam" and through Salisbury, leaving half of the town in each county.) John Caldwell and the commissioners chose a spot for their town on the east bank of the Wicomico River on the land of William Winder, a minor. The spot was also on the north side of land subsequently patented by Caldwell and was close by the private plantation of the Lords Baltimore, containing 6,000 acres of which Caldwell was the steward. The original town was laid out in 25 lots on 15 acres. In 1763, a petition was sent to the legislature to increase the size of the town to 50 acres, all to come out of William Winder's property. The bill passed the House of Delegates, but, when it was sent to the state senate, it was marked "will not pass." William Winder, who, in 1763, was an adult and a prominent citizen, did not sign the petition.

Caldwell built his mill dam in 1738 over the east branch of the Wicomico and, in 1741, built a bridge over the north branch of the river. By the time he died in 1747, he had attracted all the businesses and crafts necessary for a prosperous town.

After Caldwell's death, the leaders of Salisbury were forced to focus on the development of business in order to attract people to their town. They did it so well that Salisbury became the business center of the bi-county area by the time of the Civil War. A devastating fire in 1860 failed to prostrate Salisbury. The arrival of the railroad and the outbreak of war, which served to stop construction of the railroad, left Salisbury as the railhead during the war years. This meant that all foodstuffs and lumber had to be hauled to Salisbury to be shipped north. It made Salisbury the distribution point for goods coming south, an advantage that Salisbury has never relinquished through the years.

Then, in 1867, Salisbury's leaders started a revolt that led to the establishment of another county, Wicomico. With Salisbury as its county seat and with the establishment of newspapers here, Wicomico became the shopping center for the lower shore. The establishment of the hospital in Salisbury, the first hospital outside of Baltimore, brought medical attention here and continued Salisbury's leadership. In 1925, the establishment of a normal school made Salisbury an educational leader, as well.

Even disaster spurred development: the breach of the mill dam on Division Street led to the development of East Main Street and the Park.

Finally, Salisbury has become a communication center (with radio, television, and newspapers with wide circulations, all with appeal well beyond city limits) and a financial center (with banks, local and regional, in profusion). Our Normal School has become a university, our railhead has turned into an airport and a trucking center, and Main Street has changed from a street where you bought clothes and food to a street devoted primarily to lawyer's offices, radio and television stations, and business offices.

Today, Salisbury has a daily working and shopping population in excess of 50,000 souls. It is now a mini-colossus where people of all races live, work, and worship in reasonable harmony.

This book will tell you, by means of the postcard, how some of this took place. The postcard became popular in America with the Colombian Exposition in 1893, and, by 1900, there were postcards everywhere featuring scenes of everything. In 1907, a shop devoted to the sale of postcards opened in Salisbury and bragged that it had 100,000 cards in stock. It began to produce views of Salisbury and the surrounding towns and even had its own logo printed on the backs of cards. It is shown here.

Postcards of local scenes, groups, and events have been and are being produced in profusion, and the saving and collecting of them is what made this book possible. A postcard club has been formed, and this book is dedicated to the Delmarva Postcard Club, which meets at the library on the second Monday of each month. Our library sits on the site that was once occupied by John Caldwell's mill, the subject of the first picture of this book.

All postcards are from the collection of the author unless credit is attributed to the lender.

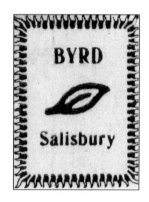

One
THE MILL DAMS

Salisbury was built around three mill ponds. Grinding corn and wheat and sawing timber were its core businesses (later wool carding was added, but this was incidental). By the last decade of the 19th century, only the grinding of corn by waterpower was still left. Water-powered mills, with their quiet gurgle as water rushed over the spillway, no longer furnished enough speed and power. Steam and electricity made the mill pond obsolete or only a bit of the scenery. The mill dam on Division Street was important because of its use as a means for horse-drawn vehicles to get to and from Salisbury. With the advent of the automobile, it became too narrow, and, when it collapsed in 1909, the mill dam was not rebuilt. The dam on Parsons Road has been out of use for so long that no one even remembers it. The dam off Isabella Street was never a roadway, so it became memorable only when it gave way and washed out Isabella Street below it.

THE OLD MILL. This picture, entitled "The Old Mill," is one of Division Street. It gives an air of isolation that is deceiving. It was taken at high tide on a summer day and shows a man poling a skiff. There is no intimation that a busy artery of traffic is only 50 feet away.

A Scene at the Head of the Wicomico River. This picture was taken 100 feet further away from the mill dam than the previous one, still showing a man and skiff. The flour mill is on the left where it cannot be seen but a portion of the roadway appears at the right.

THE SOUTH BRANCH OF THE WICOMICO RIVER, WHERE THE TIDE RISES HIGH. This scene is about 150 yards from Division Street, shown by the line of houses. The flour mill is to the left and the sawmill to the right with the dam between them. The mill owner's house is the square building near the flour mill. Market Street is presently on the left; Carroll Street is to the right.

THE RUINS OF AN OLD MILL. The old water tower can be seen in the background, and the wooden Camden Street bridge is in the foreground. The mill to the right is the ruins of the Lime Mill on the Camden side of the river. It was originally built to burn oyster shells but, by 1840, was burning crushed limestone. (Collection of Wicomico County Free Library.)

THE OLD MILL DAM. This shows what the mill dam on Division Street looked like in its last days. This picture was taken after the high school at Upton Street opened. Notice the sidewalk on the east side and the line of telephone poles on the west. The trees had been growing on the dam for at least 150 years in 1905.

LOCUST GROVE. This is the mill owner's house. It was probably built about 1820 by the Reverend James Laird, who had married a daughter of William Winder Jr., the previous operator. Gen. Thomas Humphreys bought the mill from Laird. At the time of this picture, it was the home of Mayor Thomas Humphreys, Salisbury's second mayor. The Humphreys family had owned the mill for about 100 years in 1905. The pond, known as Humphreys Lake, extended for over a mile from the dam, and downtown Salisbury, up to present Route 13, is all located on recovered pond bottom. The dam on the north prong of the river was the second dam built in Salisbury. It was built by Littleton Dennis and Josiah Polk about 1760. Dennis died, and Polk bought his interest from his widow. When Polk died, he left the mill to his sister, Sarah Bailey, who conveyed it to her son. The Humphreys brothers bought it from him. When they divided their properties, Dr. Cathell Humphreys got this mill and Gen. Humphreys got Wicomico Falls.

WICOMICO FALLS. This mill dam is built of rocks and had only a walkway across it. The lumber mill was served by a separate access road from the west, and Isabella Street dead-ended at the wool carding mill and the gristmill on the east. The peninsula by the lumber mill was used as a drying place for the sawn lumber. The large building below the gristmill was the planing mill with its drying sheds.

WICOMICO FALLS. This is a closer look. Here you can see the walkway. The shelf-like way below the dam was for a horse or a horse and rider. You can also see why this dam was called "Tumblin' Dam" by local citizens.

THE HEADWATERS OF THE NORTH BRANCH. This scene is north of Deer's Head Hospital and is probably near Naylor Mill Road.

Two
THE OYSTER SHELL ERA

Salisbury suffered a crippling fire in its downtown area in 1886 that leveled nearly all the buildings between the north prong of the river and Division Street. The town then decreed that the downtown area could only be rebuilt with brick or stone. By 1900, most of the downtown area had been rebuilt, and people were ready for all the modern improvements that were then becoming available. Telephone service began when a line was strung from the railroad station to the William B. Tilghman Co. office, and by 1902 there were 211 telephones in Salisbury. The first electrical generating plant was located near the standpipe, but it burned. In 1900, a new plant was erected at the site of the gristmill on Isabella Street, and its generators were run by waterpower. Finally, a new plant was built on Mill Street not far from its predecessor. The Camden Sewer Company was chartered in 1904 to collect and dump raw sewage into the harbor. The Home Gas Co. was organized in 1908. The city required it to furnish gas free to all municipal buildings as a condition of its franchise. All of these services were, at sometime, under local ownership. Led by the Jackson family, local leaders were determined that Salisbury, with a population of 4,277 in 1900, should come into the 20th century with all the modern conveniences, and they opened their wallets to provide them.

MAIN STREET FROM PIVOT BRIDGE. This picture was taken between 1901 and 1903. Notice the three poles shown. The closest on the left, which has one arm and two glass bells, is the telephone pole. The pole in the rear bears a street light that can be raised and lowered. Now examine the next picture.

THE CITY HALL AND FIREHOUSE. It was built in 1896. The first floor was the firehouse; the stables were in back. The town offices and the council chamber were on the second floor. Fire hoses came in 60-foot lengths, and so the tower was designed to be tall enough to hang a hose up to dry after each use.

SOUTH MAIN STREET. This is the same scene minus the poles. Frank Todd's wholesale grocery is at left, with Doody Bros. next door. The Merchant's Hotel is on the opposite corner of Mill Street. The Farmers and Planters building is on the right, followed by a wholesale candy company and the Jackson Brothers Co. on the corner of Dock Street. On August 24, 1901, the newspaper reported that terra-cotta pipes had been buried in the gutter to carry off storm water and that they were covered with crushed stone. You can see the platforms across the pipe. The street is unpaved.

MAIN STREET LOOKING WEST. This postcard shows the center of the blocks on Main Street around the same time. The Adams Express Co. owned the two delivery wagons, and their office was on the south side of the street. The two parallel lines across the street are a walkway for pedestrians to cross the dirt street. It was built at the highest point on the street.

MAIN STREET FROM DIVISION. The telephone poles have only one cross arm; the second pole bears a street light. Construction of the Wicomico News Building on the far right was begun in April 1899. It was a joint project by the contractor and the principal user, the Brewington brothers of the *News*. Daniel Cannon's cigar manufactory is in the shop under the awning, and a grocery store is next door.

MAIN STREET LOOKING EAST. The view is before 1905; the street is dirt. The Levi N. Parsons Building would be torn down in turn in the early 1920s, and East Main Street extended to the railroad embankment and to Cathell Street.

THE SALISBURY HOTEL. The hotel was built on Railroad Avenue adjacent to the station. It served the passengers on the railroad, particularly the drummers, or salesmen, who came by train and hired carriages to call on their customers. When Simon Ulman first came to Salisbury, he had a carriage for hire providing service between the hotel and downtown Salisbury. This picture dates from the 1880s, when D.C. Adams was operating the hotel. (Collection of Dr. Laurence Claggett.)

Three
BIRD'S-EYE VIEWS

The first of these bird's-eye views of Salisbury were taken by T.H. Fowler in 1906 in preparation for the lithographic view of Salisbury, which had been commissioned by Byrd, a postcard dealer. Byrd decided to publish the views separately on postcards, thus getting double dollars for his venture. The views were all taken from the water tower located behind the Parsons Home. There is some overlap, as would be expected, since the photographs were to be used in the compilation of a lithographic view of the town. Apparently, these cards were very popular. They were reissued on August 24, 1907, by Byrd and reprinted by J.G. McCrorey in 1908. When these were reissued, the scenes were numbered differently, so pay no attention to the numbers on the cards. The airplane was also the best way to show the growth of Salisbury, and Walter Thurston became the man to document it. The last two pictures are his work. These pictures require close attention in order to see what each reveals. The last picture in this section is the last one taken from a stationary object. It shows how much can be hidden by trees.

SCENE NO. 1. The Bell Street School is at the lower right with the Chestnut Street School behind it. On the left side of the picture is Park Avenue with West Chestnut Street crossing its dead end to form a "T." The house shown facing the dead end was the home of Miss Julia Todd, and the house facing Park Avenue was the home of Mrs. Emma Lou Smith. The very large house in the central part of the picture was the home of State Senator Disharoon and is on the corner of Division Street and Isabella. (Collection of Jessica Anderson.)

SCENE NO. 2. Asbury Church commands the center of the card with its parsonage, shown with the round tower, opposite. The Irving Powell House is on the north corner of Chestnut; the house on the south corner is no longer standing. The Presbyterian church can be seen behind Asbury. Notice the windmill next to the church.

SCENE NO. 3. The houses in the foreground whose backs are visible on High Street are still there. Trinity Methodist's new church is at left center with its bell tower in front of the power lines on Division Street. On the east side of Division and to the right of Trinity are the R.E. Powell and the W.C. Guilett Houses, with the Dr. Charles Fisher and the Levin W.Dorman Houses opposite them. These four houses are now part of the U.S. 50 right-of-way. The Central Hotel and the Orient Hotel were on Church and Water Streets and have both disappeared, along with the Methodist Episcopal South Church, later St. Francis de Sales. Notice the railroad trestle across Humphreys's Lake. The new high school is in the trees behind the church spire. The courthouse is barely in the picture at right.

SCENE NO. 4. The left side of this picture is a repeat of the last one. The courthouse is at right center with the Masonic Temple to its right; the high school is behind them. You get a good view of south Salisbury.

SCENE NO. 5. The courthouse is at left with the Masonic Temple opposite it. The city hall and firehouse, with its hose-drying tower, are behind the temple. St. Peter's Church, without its bell tower, is in the center. The Gunby Building is visible on the south side of Main Street, and the Peninsula Hotel is the large building at right. The large building with a tower to the right of city hall is the Wicomico News Building, and the light-colored building with a roof is the Humphreys Mill. The two buildings whose backs are to the camera are on the east side of Church Street, and the house closest to the camera is on High Street. They have disappeared due to Route 50.

SCENE NO. 6. All of Fulton Station is shown. The two-story building with the sheds attached is still there. Mill Street is visible with a line of power poles in the street and a line of rail cars opposite. Parsons's liquor store is shown between Church and High Streets with the Farmers & Planters Building to the south of it. Dock Street cuts to the left, south of Parsons's store, and the Dorman & Smith Building is on its north side with the B.L. Gillis Building (now Feldman's) on its south. The John Williams lumber mill is on the Camden side of the river, and Mitchell's Planing & Millwork Plant is on the south side of the east branch of the Wicomico.

An Aerial View. This view, from the mid-1920s, was taken from the hotel looking north on Division Street. On the left is the Masonic Temple, then the Williams Building, then the Cimino Building, and then Fooks's grocery store. On the right, obscured by trees, is the courthouse, and, behind it, on the corner, is the Hodgson Building with the George Hill Funeral Home to the right of it. Behind that is the William Penn Hotel, and in the background is the Gullett residence. To the right of the William Penn Hotel is the Central Hotel and Bond Street, with a brick block of stores and apartments west of Broad Street. The buildings on the right were torn down either for Route 50 or for the government office building. (Collection of James Jackson.)

An Aeroplane View of Salisbury. This picture was taken before the Mill Street Bridge was built and Route 50 was run through Salisbury. The First Shore Federal Building has not been erected nor has the municipal parking lot been cleared.

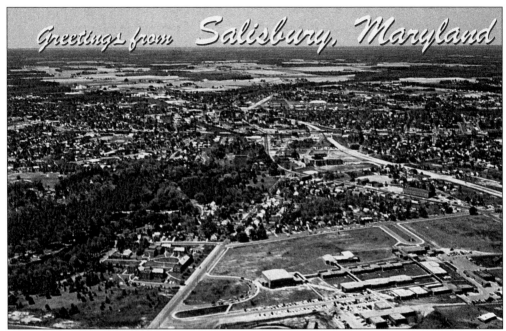

GREETINGS FROM SALISBURY, MARYLAND. This picture was taken from the east. Wicomico High School is in the foreground. The east branch of the river winds through the park on the left. This view shows the railroad and Route 13 as a straight slash in the middle background.

AN AERIAL OF SALISBURY. Now the view has been expanded to show a greater area. The Circle Avenue bridge and the parking garage have been built, but the Wicomico Theater and the old Division Street bridge still stand. The new addition to the hospital has not yet been built.

Four

ON THE YELLOW
BRICK ROAD

The first hard-surfaced street paving took place in the spring of 1904. The paving material was made of vitrified yellow bricks on a concrete base. It was truly Salisbury's "yellow brick road" and remained so for many years. It began at the pivot bridge, ran up Main Street to Division, made a left turn on Division, went one block to Church, made a right turn on Church, and then ran to the N.Y.P. & N. Railway track. The road cost $27,800, or $8 per running foot, of which the Town paid one-half and the abutting property owners on each side paid one-quarter. No advance thought had been given, however, to the noise level made by the grinding of the iron wheel rims on the brick, and the clop-clop of the horses' hooves. The town council opted for macadam for the next streets that were paved. In this chapter, you will be shown the scenes on the yellow brick road, going from west to east, and then the individual buildings or interiors abutting it.

THE PIVOT BRIDGE. The pivot bridge replaced the high-arched fixed bridge across the river and made the Jackson lumber mill feasible. A pivot bridge restricted the size of the opening, and the ram was designed to navigate through it. W.E. Sheppard & Co. bought Frank Todd's wholesale grocery business in 1906. (Collection of Jessica Anderson.)

MAIN STREET LOOKING EAST. Dock Street is on the right, and in front of it is the public drinking fountain from an artesian well with a man bent over it getting a drink. He is in the shadow of the Jackson Building. On the opposite side is the first motorcycle in Salisbury; it belonged to Morrison Tull. The "Smoke House" sign was also a first—the first electric sign. The "Watson's" sign above it is unlit. George Phipps's jewelry store is next and then the Surprise store, the town's tallest building. The time is 1910.

MAIN STREET. This picture is earlier, and there is no Surprise Store. Lacy Thoroughgood started in business in 1887, as did Charles F. Bethke, the merchant tailor whose sign is at left. H.W. Todd split from his brother Frank and was in the wholesale tobacco business. The vertical sign attached to the building in the foreground belongs to Twilley and Hearn, who advertised hot and cold baths and shoe shines each for a nickel. The time is about 1906.

THE DORMAN & SMYTHE HARDWARE CO. The hardware business was started by Levin W. Dorman, and he built the building in 1886. Smythe was in the business for only a short time. The company bragged that it had nearly 12,000 square feet under its roof. Richard Leviness, a Dorman grandson, was operating the business when it closed during the Depression. The building was taken over by the Thomas R. Young Music Store. It has been vacant since that business closed a decade ago.

ULMAN'S GRAND OPERA HOUSE. The Ulman brothers, Simon and Isaac, came to Salisbury in 1868. They were the first Jewish people to become part of the civic and business life of the community. They built this building in 1889 and had a saloon and a wholesale liquor business on the ground floor until local option closed it in 1900. From then on, they operated a furniture, carpet, and variety store. They commissioned and sold postcards of Salisbury for many years. The second floor contained the movie theatre auditorium. It was the first place in Salisbury with permanent seating and was therefore used for high school graduations, plays, and the dedication ceremonies for Peninsula General Hospital. The building burned in 1968 and was not rebuilt. This picture was taken before 1907, when an electric sign was installed. (Collection of E. Pusey.)

THE MODEL VARIETY STORE. The picture is of Thomas Steele & Co. trading as the Model Variety Store. This building was originally the Brewington Building, which was built by H.S. Brewington, the hatter. Steele occupied the center of these units only for a few years, beginning in April 1914. The entire building was taken over by Woolworth's in 1919 and was operated by them for about 70 years. It has now been completely remodeled and is used by the Arts Center and other offices.

MAIN STREET SHOWING THE ARCADE THEATER. The Arcade Theater was opened on December 31, 1914. It showed movies and also had vaudeville shows. The Arcade could also be rented for community activities. The Schine Theater Co. finally operated it. It caught fire and burned down in the 1940s and was replaced by the Read Drug Store. The building is now the home of television station WMDT.

THE FARMERS AND MERCHANTS BANK (RIGHT) AND THE SALISBURY NATIONAL BANK. These buildings were built only a few months apart in 1904. The Salisbury National opened in 1884 and the Farmers and Merchants in 1893. Both banks had outgrew their previous quarters and each commissioned a new building, only a few doors apart and both on the south side of Main Street. The Salisbury National, as befitted the oldest bank, had a 26-foot-high ceiling, a marble floor, and mahogany woodwork. The Farmers and Merchants Bank had only tile floors and oak woodwork. They both continued to grow and prosper.

THE L.W. GUNBY HARDWARE CO. This building has been completely remodeled along with the building on its east side. In the process, the building lost its distinctive roof line, architecture, and third-floor display window. It was built in 1886 by Gunby to replace his burned store on the same site. Gunby was enormously successful, and this retail operation was his anchor store. After his death, it was rented to a retail clothing chain, then sold and converted into offices with a restaurant in the basement. It is now a walk-through building with offices and stores on either side and a large roof over its lower level in the rear, covering the entire street.

MAIN STREET LOOKING WEST. This is probably the first picture showing the yellow brick road. The concrete pavements have also been poured, but notice the number of grates that have been put in for light and air to the basements. On the right is a permanent awning with plain pipe legs. The water company was the tenant here. The time is about 1906.

Main Street from Division Street, Salisbury, Md.

MAIN STREET FROM DIVISION STREET. The Columbian National Life Insurance Co. had their offices in the corner building on the left, as did William S. Gordy, who was also an insurance agent. C.T. Layfield, a merchant tailor, had his shop on the first floor. Samuel S. Woodcock, a real estate broker, had the last office in the corner building. Dr. Slemons, who was also the clerk of court, had his home and office in the second building. On the north side of the street was the men's wear store of Leonard H. Higgins, *c.* 1908.

FAIR DAY IN SALISBURY. It is obviously summer. The only fair that Salisbury celebrated was the "Whitsunday Fair." Toulson's Drug Store did not open until 1907. The printing of the Toulson signs is obviously amateur, which leads to the conclusion that this was at least a circus day. A circus may have been scheduled on Fair Day. This card was mailed out for Christmas in 1911, but the scene is earlier.

THE PALM GARDEN. This was located on the north side of Main, east of St. Peter Street. G.A. Wilson, the former owner, successfully sold stock in the company. There were 80 stockholders, and Raymond K. Truitt, Dr. J. McFadden Dick, B. Frank Kennerly, G. William Phillips, William B. Tilghman Jr., Henry B. Freeny, and J.R. White were the directors. They were the most prominent young men in town in 1909. It took them all of a year to learn that you could not pay bills with ice cream. It was succeeded by The Fountain Cafe. (Collection of James Jackson.)

THE FOUNTAIN CAFE. The Fountain Cafe succeeded the Palm Garden after it was completely remodeled. It started as only a soda fountain but began to serve meals in 1910. The building was later sold to the Collier Drug Co.

THE STORE OF HARPER & TAYLOR. This store was refixtured in 1901 and was, as it appears on the postcard, the most modern jewelry store in town. It was on the north side of Main Street. It was succeeded by John Kuhn, who bought the business. Charles Harper was the mayor of Salisbury from 1904 to 1910 and the harbor master after that. (Collection of Dr. Laurence Claggett.)

THE CORNER OF MAIN AND DIVISION STREETS. This picture was taken at a time when parking on the south side of Main Street was allowed. The Salisbury Building & Loan Association occupied the first floor of the building on the right, then the Peoples Bank took over. The upper floors were for offices. On Main Street, the first building shown is the Whealton Building, the second is the Salisbury Times Building, and the third is the Brewington Building. On South Division, the first office is that of Franklyn Woodcock, a real estate broker. The next building housed the office of L. Atwood Bennett, an attorney, and other offices were upstairs. Camden Street is next, and the building shown here was built to house a Gunby automobile franchise. The time is about World War I.

THE WICOMICO COUNTY COURTHOUSE. The courthouse was built in 1872 to house the county offices and the courtroom. Originally, there was a cross corridor on the first floor with an outside door on each side and a single door in front. As government business increased and more space was needed, the cross corridors were eliminated, and a second door was added in front. The outside steps, however, were left in place.

THE MASONIC TEMPLE. We can pinpoint that this picture was taken in November 1904. The trees are bare; the pavement in front of the temple has not yet been laid. Neither of the tenants on the first floor have moved in. The Jay Williams Building on the right is still a two-story building—there are window blinds on only half the windows on the third floor. The lodge bought the property in 1903, let the contract for the building in April 1904, held the cornerstone ceremonies in late May, and expected the building to be completed in November. The post office was to move in on the first of October but didn't quite make it. But the brick paving is complete, and look at the telephone pole.

A CARD ENTITLED "WICOMICO HIGH SCHOOL." The title is a mistake. They meant the Salisbury College of Business. The fire escape was added in June 1909 to meet the requirements of the fire code. The Jay Williams Building now has a third floor. The paving line on the yellow brick road is visible where it joins the dirt Water (now Calvert) Street.

THE CHANTRY HOUSE. Beulah and Dorothy White bought the property when it was built in 1925. They operated the hotel and restaurant until 1932, when the mortgage was foreclosed. The Chantry House continued to operate under new owners until it was sold to the county as part of the land for the government office building.

THE FRONT DINING ROOM OF THE BLUE BIRD TEA ROOM. This was on the second floor of the Cimino Building on the west side of Division Street, north of the Jay Williams Building. It was quite successful, and the White sisters, who operated it, opened another tea room in Ocean City. Their first success, however, led them to the eventual failure of the Chantry House.

THE SALISBURY HARDWARE CO. The Salisbury Hardware Co. was at the end of the yellow brick road. The railroad extended the road by paving the block between William and Isabella on Railroad Avenue with yellow brick. This building was located on the northwest corner of Church, William, and Railroad Avenue. The passenger station was at Isabella and Railroad Avenue.

Five

NICE NEIGHBORHOODS

In 1900, there were two nice neighborhoods in Salisbury, Newtown and Camden. Newtown is the oldest. It was laid out in lots by a Dr. Haney from land on the Somerset side of Dividing Street; the north boundary was where the B.C. & A. tracks are now. There were two lots on the Worcester side that were sold off by Levin Handy before Dr. John Huston bought the property. This land was separated from Salisbury by the Nelms property on the Somerset side and the Fooks and Huston properties on the Worcester side. When houses were built on the lots, the New Town was separate from the Old Town, and the name stuck. Camden got its name from the plat of Sally Hooper, the developer. She bought the land from the estate of her father and laid the land out on both sides of Chestnut Street, in order to, as she described it, "meet the proposed new bridge over the Wicomico." The name comes from the Battle of Camden, in which many Salisburians had fought under the command of General Greene. Division Street (north to the B.C. & A. railroad tracks) and Camden Street (south to Winder Street) were in the second lot of streets to be paved—with macadam.

Division St. from Church St. looking N., Salisbury, Md.

DIVISION STREET FROM CHURCH. The houses on both sides of the street are now part of the bed of U.S. 50. The house on the right is the house of W.C. Gullett. Next to it is the home of R.E. Powell. On the left just barely visible are the homes of Dr. Charles P. Fisher and Levin W. Dorman. Division Street is paved, which dates the picture to 1908.

THE R.E. POWELL HOUSE. There was an earlier house on the site, but it was burned in 1886. This was the only place where the fire crossed Division Street. The new house was completed in 1889, had speaking tubes in every room, and frescoing by an artist from Wilmington. Its outside privy was not burned and has been moved to Poplar Hill Mansion. The privy was no longer used and the house was connected to the new sewer that ran north on Division Street to Isabella.

WILLIAM STREET FROM DIVISION. The Grier-Gillis House steps can be seen at left. On the right is the Arthur Leonard House, which has been replaced by the John Downing House. Behind it is the Walter Disharoon House, which has forms in front of it for a new sidewalk. The trees at right are still in the street.

William Street, Salisbury, Md.

WILLIAM STREET WEST FROM POPLAR HILL. The porch on the house on the left is still there; behind it is the Perry-Cooper House, which has been magnificently restored. Next is Gay Street, a one-block street. On the right, the house is still there, but unrestored. Next to that is the Robert Ellegood House and beyond that the Jay Williams House looking down Gay. William Street was paved from Division to Poplar Hill in 1908, but here it is unpaved. There is a paved crossover at the corner, however.

WILLIAM STREET. The Leonard House on the left was built before the street was cut through in 1902. Bethesda Church has not yet been built on the lot to the right. The two houses on the left on Park Street have been built, but the house that now stands on the northeast corner of Park Street has not. The street has yet to be paved. The time is about 1910.

Isabella Street, from Division St., Salisbury, Md.

ISABELLA FROM DIVISION. On the left on the corner is the F.A. Grier House. Next to that is the Augustus G. Toadvine House, which, when built, was on a lot that occupied the whole corner, and its lot extended back to Elizabeth Street. It has recently been restored. The house on the right side was replaced by the Dr. Dick House. Isabella is unpaved, but the paving extends far enough back to offer a paved walkway.

THE FRED GRIER HOUSE. This picture was taken on the Fourth of July, and the families posed on the front steps. The trees in front have been whitewashed.

NORTH DIVISION STREET. This picture is much later, and the trees are gone. William Street is to the south. The Leonard House and the Bethesda Methodist Church are on the right corner. On the left are the Arthur Leonard House, which has now been torn down, and the Grier-Gillis House on the north side. The time is at least 1930.

AN UNIDENTIFIED CAR OWNER. This picture was taken on Poplar Hill Avenue. The house on the left was built by Alfonso Wootten after his sale of the Victor Lynn Lines. It is flanked by three row houses, which are very unique in Salisbury.

THE HOUSE OF CHARLES R. DISHAROON. This house is on the southwest corner of Isabella Street and North Division and was built around the turn of the century. Disharoon joined the E.S. Adkins Co. in 1896, but he withdrew and, in 1906, started his own company called the Salisbury Crate and Barrel Company. Disharoon was the mayor of Salisbury from 1900 to 1904 and the state senator for Wicomico from 1922 to 1926. (Collection of Dr. Laurence Claggett.)

THE RESIDENCE OF THE LATE FORMER-GOVERNOR E.E. JACKSON. This mansion was surrounded by a brick wall and occupied an entire block. It was surrounded on two sides by the B.C. & A. Railroad tracks, and, on the remaining two, by Division and Isabella Streets. The governor was one of the richest men in Salisbury. He had a lumber mill on Mill Street and would drive sedately down a road paved with oyster shells (which he had paid for) to his mill. His mansion was built around 1880 on the same site the militia had used for training. The mansion has now been torn down and replaced by an entire development.

Salisbury, Maryland

THE PERRY-COOPER HOUSE AND THE POPLAR HILL MANSION. The Perry-Cooper House is on the south side of William. It was built around 1880 and has been meticulously restored. It is entirely surrounded by attractive picket fencing, and the house is painted a dark burgundy red. The Poplar Hill Mansion was the original home of Dr. John Huston, who resided on the east side of North Division Street. It was begun by Maj. Levin Handy and finished by Huston. Originally, the mansion had a semi-detached kitchen wing on the rear. It is now owned by the City of Salisbury and run by a separate board. The mansion is nearly self-supporting and is available for rent for parties and weddings.

Camden Avenue, Salisbury, Md.

CAMDEN AVENUE. The picture is one of peace and serenity. The spiked fence on the left indicated the Jackson properties. The house on the right is no longer there but was once the property of H.L. Gillis. The lot in the foreground is that of L.W. Gunby. The street is paved.

CAMDEN AVENUE. The left foreground of this picture shows the L.M. Dashiell House, then Newton Street and the Newton Jackson property. The house on the right was the home of Col. Samuel A. Graham.

THE RESIDENCE OF WILLIAM H. JACKSON. This was the house of Congressman William H. Jackson. He felt that he had to match the mansion of his older brother and former partner, the governor. The congressman's mansion was an imposing house built in the Queen Anne style and completed in 1891. From a description of the house in the newspaper comes this statement: "It contains one of the coziest dens imaginable and will be used by Mr. Jackson as a smoking apartment." The house was loaned by the St. Francis Catholic Church during World War II to be used as the local United Service Organization. The house burned down and was eventually replaced by a parochial school.

W.P. JACKSON'S RESIDENCE. The house of Senator William P. Jackson was a replica of his father's house next door, except that it was finished in a slightly grander style, with silver-plated door hinges, for example. Jackson was appointed to the U.S. Senate to finish the term of a deceased senator. He did not, however, run for reelection. The house was bought by the late Henry Roberts to be used for his office and, after his death, was bought by the Catholic Church. They used the house as a rectory for a while, but it was finally torn down and replaced with a new, somewhat smaller building also used as a rectory.

CAMDEN AVENUE BOULEVARD. The first house built on either side of Camden Avenue was situated around Pennsylvania and Virginia Avenues on the west side and North Boulevard on the east side. Camden Avenue was still unpaved. The trees on the near side have obviously been planted. The house belonged to Col. Marion A. Humphreys. It is identifiable by the two dormer windows on the third floor, the wrap-around porch, and the two large columns in front. The time is 1913.

Camden Avenue from North Boulevard,
Salisbury, Md.

CAMDEN AVENUE FROM NORTH BOULEVARD. Camden Avenue has now been paved, and "millionaire's row" has been built. The first house built, then occupied by Jesse D. Price, is at right. The second house belonged to Capt. John Hagen, followed by the house built on the south side of Virginia for Mrs. Levin D. Collier by her father as a wedding present. It costs more to paint these houses now than it originally did to build them.

RESIDENTIAL SECTION. This picture, taken from the south end of "millionaire's row," shows the Collier House in the foreground, then Virginia Avenue. Next is the Hagen House with its windmill, and the Humphreys House in the distance. The three houses all had wrap-around porches and big columns in front.

CAMDEN AVENUE LOOKING SOUTH. We have covered "millionaire's row" on the right side of the street, but the houses on the left are also of interest. The house on the corner of North Boulevard was the home of Judge Levin Claude Bailey, and the building next to it was converted 50 years ago to the Ludlam Apartments. The time is about 1915.

Residence of W. F. Allen, near Salisbury, Md.

THE RESIDENCE OF W.F. ALLEN. This house was built in 1904 on land that is now part of the campus of Salisbury State University. It contained 12 rooms. The barn shown in the rear cost $4,000. The water tank held 28,000 gallons, was 95 feet high, and was used to irrigate the crops on Allen's entire farm, which extended well across Camden Avenue. At the time, he claimed to be the largest grower of strawberry plants in the world. The house was torn down by the university, and the land is now part of the campus.

NEWTON STREET. The bicyclist in this picture is enjoying the paved street. This was the other street laid out by Mrs. Hooper in 1838. At the end of the street is the Graham House. The second house on the left on Newton Street was the home of Judge E. Stanley Toadvine. The mailbox is no longer there, but it marked the beginning of Light Street.

Six

RIVER SCENES

The Wicomico River has always played an important role in the history of Salisbury (which was originally called Handy's Landing). As you can tell from the early pictures of the harbor, the age of gasoline and the age of sail are somewhat mixed together. At one time, the harbor silted up so badly that steamers could not get into Salisbury but had to stop at either Cotton Patch Wharf or Shad Point. Merchandise had to be poled up on shallow draft bateaux to the merchants' stores. In 1888, the river was dredged to a depth of 9 feet up to the Main Street Bridge. In 1931, the channel was dredged to a 13-foot depth at mean low tide, and this depth has been maintained. Salisbury has been Maryland's second port for many years. A committee has even been formed to see that, in winter, the river is free of ice and remains navigable. At one time, a canal existed between the Main and Camden Street Bridges to serve the merchants whose stores fronted on Main. The canal ran east past Market Street and, when Market Street was cut through to Camden Bridge, the bridge commission had to pay to have the canal filled. An active shipbuilding industry, the oldest business in Salisbury, has been maintained in the town from before the Revolution up to the present. The Chris-Craft factory was located in Salisbury because of the large reservoir of men here who were familiar with boats and their manufacture.

BOAT WHARF. This picture is of the boat landing on West Main Street where the *Virginia* tied up. The water tower can be seen in the background. The time is 1910.

WICOMICO HARBOR. The two boys on the boat are Franklyn Woodcock and Jack Gunby (the son of L.W. Gunby), and the man standing up in the boat is Samuel Woodcock, a real estate dealer. The picture was taken from the Camden Street Bridge; the Gillis warehouse is on the right (where Feldman's is now). The line of houses in the background marks West Main Street.

Steamboat "Virginia," Salisbury, Md.

THE STEAMBOAT *VIRGINIA*. This picture was taken from the tip of Coxon's Island across the river. This island was high land on the river's edge with the cripples behind it. The sheds from the preceding picture are shown here.

F. A. Grier & Son, Salisbury Machine Shops, Salisbury, Md.

F.A. GRIER & SON. The Grier brothers came to Salisbury after the 1886 fire and went into business together. Eventually, they separated and Fred Grier and his son went into the machine shop and boat engine-repair business on the river.

THE WICOMICO RIVER. This picture was taken from Camden Bridge. The harbor is less crowded now; only one sailboat is left. You can now see the main body of the river on your left, and the east branch is in the foreground. The Sash & Door Co. is still at left, and the houses on West Main Street are still there. The shed of the *Virginia*'s dock is on the opposite side of the river. The Gillis warehouse is still in place, but a brick building has been built along side it with a protruding beam near the roof line for a rope to haul freight up to each of the three platforms. The time is 1922.

THE MAIN STREET BRIDGE AND HARBOR IN WYCOMICO. This picture was made before Route 50 was built. The *Virginia* was still running, and the Victor Lynn line was operating from the dock on the opposite side of the river. The lumber yard was also still in operation (as shown by the stacks of lumber visible in the background). Notice the different spelling of Wycomico.

54

THE HARBOR. This picture looks upriver. The Main Street Bridge is at left next to the white building. The Turner Bros. warehouse is next to it, and a vessel of the Victor Lynn lines is tied up at their dock. The time is about 1935.

WATERMELON BOATS. These sailboats still called at Salisbury to haul watermelons to Baltimore in the 1940s. As the watermelons were sold at auction, the growers were instructed to take their load to the harbor where it would be unloaded on a boat. As soon as the boat was fully loaded, it would cast off for Baltimore. (Collection of the late Hilda Fowler.)

THE PADDLEWHEEL QUEEN. This is the first of the cruise ships in Salisbury, but the paddlewheel is just for show. She ran down the Wicomico on regular sight-seeing cruises. Her owner went bankrupt, and she was sold. (Collection of the late Hilda Fowler.)

THE SALISBURY MARINA. This municipally owned marina dates from 1986. It is the scene of an "in-the-water boat show" held during the first week in May. The marina was also the home port of *The Maryland Lady*, the second cruise ship. This ship was sold and departed after five years on the river.

THE TURNING BASIN. This was located on the north side of the river just west of the *Virginia*'s dock. You can see, in the background, East Main Street where it is joined by Fitzwater Street. The right-angle turn of East Main Street is behind the two central trees. The house in the background at left is on the corner of Fitzwater. (Collection of Dr. Laurence Claggett.)

LAKE VIEW DAM, JOHNSON'S LAKE. This is the second dam on the site. The one shown in chapter one was washed away in 1933, and this one was built in its place, though not exactly at the same location.

LAKE VIEW PARK. This picture was taken while the original dam was still in place. You can tell by the scarcity of development on the left that it is where Parsons Cemetery is now. (Collection of the late Hilda Fowler.)

Seven

DIVINE GRACE

The history of religion in Salisbury is replete with tortuous twists and turns. At first, there were three faiths here: Anglican, Presbyterian, and Baptist. About the time of the Revolution, Methodism arrived and, in the next generation, nearly engulfed the other groups. Then, the Methodists split into so many different branches that there was a Methodist church on almost every corner. The Baptists, then, split into two churches, the Old School and the Missionary. The number of Catholics eventually became great enough to support a church, as did the number of Lutherans, Christian Scientists, and Churches of God. Area Jews rented space until 1951, when they erected a synagogue. The first church built in Salisbury was the Anglican church, built in 1769. Presbyterian services had been held at John Caldwell's mill before that, but no church had been built. The Baptists held services in Salisbury also, but these were outdoor services under an oak tree on the Nelms's property, the current site of the John B. Parsons Home. The Methodists built the little Red Meeting House on the site of Old Asbury Church on North Division Street. The Anglicans built their church on the corner of Church and St. Peter Streets and, when the church was destroyed by fire, it was rebuilt on the same site. After the 1886 fire, the bell in the church was loaned to the county, but the church asked for its return in 1997. After the bell was taken down from the courthouse tower, it was refurbished and installed in the church tower.

THE EPISCOPAL CHURCH. The first picture is of the Episcopal church with the tower only partly rebuilt. This picture was taken about 1905. In a deal the church made with the county, the church agreed that the bell would continue to toll the hours for the downtown area.

St. Peter's Episcopal Churc
Salisbury, Md.

ST. PETER'S EPISCOPAL CHURCH. This picture is notable because of the figures that have been pasted on the negative. The automobile, the boy, the man, and the woman have all been added. The parish house was not built until 1923, so it is not shown. (Collection of Wicomico County Free Library.)

THE M.E. CHURCH. This picture shows Asbury as it looked when it was first rebuilt with stone. By 1886, the congregation had outgrown the wooden church, and $6,000 had been pledged for a new one when the fire of that year burned the old one to the ground. The congregation called on William H. Jackson for help, and he said, "Build it back with stone, and I'll pay what you fall short." And he did.

THE ASBURY METHODIST CHURCH. This picture is of Asbury as it was at the time of the re-unification of the Methodist Church. The Asbury congregation decided that three Methodist churches within two blocks was too much and decided to move. They sold the Sunday school addition to the Baptists, and the rest of the church building was sold to Faith Community Church.

THE ASBURY UNITED METHODIST. In 1953, on the 175th anniversary of its founding, the Asbury United Methodist Church bought 11 acres on Camden Avenue, and a new church was finished and consecrated on May 10, 1963. A fellowship hall was added in 1968.

THE METHODIST PROTESTANT CHURCH. The Methodist Protestants date their founding to 1842. They built this church in 1872 and decided, in 1896, to name it Bethesda. The church was built on Church Street and, in 1922, the congregation ran out of room for additions so they decided to seek a new location.

BETHESDA METHODIST PROTESTANT. Property at the northwest corner of North Division and William Street was purchased by the Methodist Protestant Church, and a new church was erected and dedicated on June 3, 1923. A subsequent addition was required and, in 1926, this was added on. (Collection of Gene Wharton.)

THE TRINITY M.E. SOUTH. The Trinity M.E. Church was organized in 1866; the wife of later Governor Elihu E. Jackson was the secretary of the organizing committee. The church suffered a fire in 1884 and worshipped in the courthouse until a new church was built in 1886. The congregation outgrew this church, and the governor became the principal benefactor of a new church, also built of Port Deposit granite like the Asbury Church across the street. The church was built and dedicated on May 21, 1905. The church organ arrived by train the Monday before the dedication and was installed on the Friday before.

THE SALISBURY YOUNG MEN'S ASSOCIATION BUILDING. This building was built by Mrs. Jackson in memory of her late husband, Gov. Elihu E. Jackson. After the Young Men's Association and the YMCA (which succeeded it) failed, Mrs. Jackson gave the building to Trinity to be used for Sunday school rooms and as a place for meetings and dinners. The building is directly across the street from the church.

GRACE UNITED METHODIST. Rev. John W. Hardesty founded Grace Methodist with the assistance of William H. Jackson. Hardesty found a lot on Anne Street with a vacant run-down house on it and had Jackson lease it. In 30 days, Hardesty had the house repaired enough to use, and, on the third Sunday of October 1908, the first service was held. The church was named Grace because of Hardesty's daughter's help in its formation.

THE WICOMICO PRESBYTERIAN CHURCH.
This church traces its history to Francis
Mackemie and was one of the five original
Presbyterian Churches in the United States.
The Presbyterians built their first church in
Salisbury in 1830, and the church was
moved to this site in 1859. (*Right*) The
church only occupies a single lot. It is boxed
in by a house on both sides. In order to gain
more space, the tower was taken down, a
new one was built, and 12 feet were added to
the front of the church. (*Below*) The
building has been enlarged with a two-story
addition across the back of the church for a
Sunday school and with a single-story
addition on the right side facing the street.
The church property now goes back to
Chestnut Street.

THE DIVISION STREET BAPTIST CHURCH. The church was formed by 11 people who broke off from the Old School Baptists. These 11 people purchased the lot at the corner of East Chestnut and North Division. In 1898 they built a new church, shown here, to replace a burned one. It served until 1937. (Collection of Richard Booth.)

THE ALLEN MEMORIAL BAPTIST CHURCH. This church was rebuilt with a red-brick veneer and had a vastly different appearance. Ground was broken in 1951 for an enlarged and remodeled auditorium. The educational annex was purchased from Asbury Church in 1963. Examination of the view above will show the house that was there before and was razed. The church is now called the Allen Memorial Church.

ST. FRANCIS DE SALES CATHOLIC CHURCH, SALISBURY MD.

ST. FRANCIS DE SALES. The Catholic Church acquired this property on the corner of Calvert and Bond Streets in 1916. The house on the left was the rectory. This picture shows the building as it was. Later, the side porch was incorporated into the church.

ST. FRANCIS DE SALES. This new church was built on property donated by John E. Morris, who died a week before its dedication in 1964. Monsignor Stout was still the pastor at the time, and the building of this church was the culmination of his dream. The land for a parochial school had been purchased first. Then the rectory was added by the purchase of the William P. Jackson House, and this has been replaced, in turn, by a new rectory.

THE BETHANY LUTHERAN CHURCH. This church stands at the corner of Camden Avenue and South Boulevard. It was dedicated on May 29, 1949. The church has doubled in size since then with the addition of a fellowship building.

THE OUTDOOR CHRISTMAS PAGEANT. This was started by Rev. Oren Perdue, minister of the Salisbury Baptist Temple. It is held each year on Hobbs Road near the Baptist church. It may even be viewed from your car.

Eight

THE POND BOTTOM

On May 29, 1909, about 2 p.m., Humphreys Dam at South Division Street collapsed with a roar. What had been before a placid lake was now a pond bottom of stinking mud. The Salisbury Realty Co. purchased the property for $29,100, platted lots on the lake bottom to the railroad embankment, laid out streets, put in utilities, promoted two new bridges, and began to sell lots. The town did its part by accepting Circle Avenue, Dock Street extended, East Main Street, Baptist Street, and Water Street. The state government joined in by building new drawbridges over Camden and South Division Street, by piercing the embankment to build East Main to join Church Street and the town line, and by building an extension of the Snow Hill Road to meet East Main. The federal government cooperated by agreeing to build a new post office behind the courthouse. The public-spirited citizenry cooperated to build a new hotel, and Mayor Thomas R. Parker contributed with the purchase of most of the 60 acres beyond the railroad embankment for a city park. He paid $5,000 for the best bargain of the century.

The park houses wells and water works, tennis courts, a number of picnic areas, a former swimming area, hiking trails, a zoological park, the Winter Wonderland, the site of the Firemen's Muster, and a bandstand. At least 300,000 people a year use one or more of its facilities and attractions. Our zoo is one of Salisbury's main attractions. Christmas lights are on display each year along East Main Street, enhanced and added to every year, and the Firemen's Muster, a competition among fire companies from the entire Mid-Atlantic region, is also held here.

FIREHOUSE NUMBER ONE. The formal dedication of the first firehouse took place on February 3, 1928. John D. Lank was fire chief, and they still had an all volunteer company of 50 members. The building cost $55,000 to build.

ARMORY, CO. I. This armory was first talked about in 1912, after a fire destroyed the former armory. The state appropriated the money for the plans, and an architect designed this building, which reminds the author of a medieval castle. The building was dedicated in 1915. It was used by the state guard during World War II and was turned over to the county for use as a library after a new armory was built. It also served as state police headquarters in the early 1920s.

THE POST OFFICE. The post office was one of the first buildings in the East Main Street area. It was built in 1925, and this picture shows the original building. The murals on the interior walls were painted in 1934–35 as a Work Projects Administration (WPA) project. The old county jail is visible at the left.

THE POST OFFICE. This shows the post office after it had been enlarged. A second floor and two wings were added in 1937. The second floor was comprised of offices and a courtroom. The courtroom is used by the federal magistrate, as well as for bankruptcy hearings. The only post office business there presently is contained in a wing on the west side and boxes in the center section.

71

THE WICOMICO COUNTY COURTHOUSE. This shows the new addition added in 1936. Judges' chambers and the people's court were on the second floor, a jail occupied the third floor, and the county treasurer and the clerk of court were on the first floor. The sheriff's office and the board of election supervisors were in the basement.

MAIN STREET LOOKING WEST. The buildings on the south side are in the foreground. The Oddfellows Building, built in 1921, housed the New Theatre (which was owned by the Ulmans) on the ground floor. Next to it was the Richardson Building, built by Lloyd Richardson; next in line was the Advertiser Building, followed by the Downing Building, an all-concrete structure. (Collection of James Jackson.)

WICOMICO HOTEL
SALISBURY, MD.

WHAT WE EAT

WE ARE

❖

GOOD FOOD

MEANS

GOOD HEALTH

TYPICAL MENU: BUSINESS LUNCHEON

Cream of Celery Soup
or Cold Consomme
Choice of
Fried Filet of Sole
Corn Muffins
Braised Beef Jardiniere
Candied Sweet Potatoes
Baked Tomatoes or
Cold Sliced Ham Potato Salad
Choice of
Ice Cream,   Apple Pie
Sliced Peaches   Orange Juice
Coffee or Iced Tea
Hot Rolls or Corn Bread

50 Cents

THE WICOMICO HOTEL. The chamber of commerce commissioned a report on the feasibility of a hotel costing more than $250,000 in 1922, and the report came back saying, "Go!" In 1923, the director got an option on the land, incorporated the hotel, and all the civic leaders became stock salesmen. They first decided that the building would have five stories, but, after work started, they added two more floors to the building and started selling stock again to pay for them. The hotel was finally opened for business on October 14, 1924, and it opened with a grand celebration. This picture was made after the first addition, a canopy over the entrance on the East Main Street side, had been added. The card features a typical business luncheon menu designed to bring in local business men, and it shows the price—50¢.

THE LOBBY OF THE WICOMICO HOTEL. This card shows the lobby as it looked in its beginning. It was done with fancy plaster on the walls and ceiling and was tastefully decorated.

THE WICOMICO HOTEL, CORNER OF MAIN AND DIVISION. This picture was published 10 years later; a second canopy has been added over the Division Street entrance, and all windows on the west side now have awnings. The road markers show that Main Street was still Route 13 as far as Camden but that people wanting Route 213 had to turn right. The picture also shows that Russell White's jewelry store was located in the News Building. The most interesting thing about this picture is that, although the first traffic light had already been installed, the hand-powered stop and go kiosk had not been retired. It was still used on Saturdays and on special occasions. The kiosk sits on the courthouse corner and was mounted on wheels so that it could be easily pulled to the center of the street.

THE CONTINENTAL CAFE. The two men shown in this 1972 picture are Jean Pierre Bouvier and Jack Curtis at the time the Continental Cafe first opened in the Wicomico Hotel. The cafe continued to operate in the hotel into the 1980s, when the building ceased to be a hotel and became all offices. Today it is known as One Plaza East. (Collection of the late Hilda Fowler.)

THE SHERATON INN. This is Salisbury's only downtown hotel, looking as it did when first completed. The big sign and the drive-through registration desk are no longer there. An addition was built in 1986–87 on the end of the building and at a right angle. It is now the Ramada Inn.

BEFORE THE PARK. This picture shows how the area, now part of the park, appeared before the dam burst. The peninsula in the center is just barely visible above water, and the bluffs on the north side extend for miles.

THE WATER WORKS. New wells and a pumping station were among the first requirements of the city. The park satisfied this need. The contract for this pumping station was let in October 1925. The pumps could pump 9,500 gallons per minute. New mains were put in, providing service in East Salisbury. Notice the fill put in around the building. (Collection of Wicomico County Free Library.)

ELECTRIC FOUNTAIN, MUNICIPAL PARK, SALISBURY, MD.

THE ELECTRIC FOUNTAIN. The electric fountain was put in as one of the show-off features of the park. The fountain displays a series of colorful lights that merge into one other. It was built prior to the bicentennial of Salisbury in 1932.

THE FALLS, MUNICIPAL PARK, SALISBURY, MD.

THE FALLS. This bridge was swept away in a 1933 storm that cleared all the bridges across Beaver Dam Creek.

BATHING IN MUNICIPAL PARK. Bathing was not only permitted in the park, it was encouraged at first before pollution became an issue.

MUNICIPAL PARK. The bandstand goes back to the WPA days. The band played on the platform, and the lower level was used as a concession stand. The bandstand also acted as a podium for Vice President Nixon when he came to speak in Salisbury.

THE BRIDGE OVER THE DAM, SCHUMAKER LAKE. Bathing was eventually moved upstream, above the zoo. Then this, too, became taboo.

AROUND THE CURVE. This was another one of the bridges swept away in 1933. This bridge provided access to one of the many picnic areas in the park.

Municipal Park, Salisbury, Maryland

MUNICIPAL PARK. This bridge now carries a heavy traffic load of pedestrians at the park. It is attractive and sloped gradually to suit people of all ages. (Collection of Gene Wharton.)

WELCOME TO THE SALISBURY ZOOLOGICAL PARK. The zoo has been developing over a long period of time. Mayor Thomas R. Parker donated a couple of monkeys. A bear was donated. Then, a contest was held by the Salisbury Exchange Club in which each nickel counted as a vote, the proceeds going entirely toward the purchase of new animals. Llamas, bison, and penguins led the balloting and were added. Later, professionals were employed, and the zoo became a recognized Zoological Park. It is at the center of the park and attracts about 250,000 visitors per year.

WINTER WONDERLAND. This exhibit of lighted displays grows more ambitious each year. It is visible from East Main Street and attracts thousands of pedestrians and motorists each year at Christmastime.

THE FIREMEN'S MUSTER. Held on the second Saturday in September, the Firemen's Muster allows fire companies from the Mid-Atlantic region to gather and compete in firemen's activities.

THE ELKS CLUB. The Elks Lodge and Golf Course overlook the park and adjoin it on the south. The two, together, form an expanse of green that adds much to the landscape of the city.

THE WICOMICO YOUTH AND CIVIC CENTER. Completed in 1959, the center was financed by private subscription as a war memorial. It burned to the ground, unfortunately, but was rebuilt and enlarged with public funds. Today, it can house various attractions simultaneously and has taken care of ice shows, the Lipizzaner horses, and Loretta Lynn. It sits on the north side of the park and is a stone's throw from the zoo.

Nine

A More Modern Main Street

The end of World War I is a logical point at which to start the "more-modern" period. Parking had not yet become a problem in Salisbury. There were no visible gaps in Main Street east of Division, and the north side of the street still shielded its windows with awnings. The Model T was the car of choice, and no horse-drawn vehicles were in sight. Main Street, east of Division, was not primarily a retail clothing area but a service area, containing auto and hardware stores, restaurants, movies, the county dispensary, shirt factories, gas stations, and offices. For the next 30 years, West Main Street would be home to soft goods retailing, banks and savings and loan companies, and drug stores.

MAIN STREET. This picture is easy to date. The car on the right has a license plate bearing the year, 1922. The Brewington Building is on the left, where Woolworth's has opened. The next building has not yet been replaced by the Montgomery Ward Building (now Vernon Powell), and Ulman's has its electric sign up. The buildings on this side of the theater were occupied by J. Ryland Taylor, a printer, and C.T. Layfield, a tailor.

MAIN STREET. Western Union has moved into the Wicomico Hotel Building in this picture, and the traffic light has been installed. This indicates that the date of this picture is at least 1925. The picture shows a bay window on the second floor of White & Leonard's. The window has since been removed. Fisher's Jewelry is next, and Harold Fitch, the optician, is after that. On the opposite side of the street are Leeds and Twilley, milliners; the Bellevue Hotel; and the Salisbury Times Building. The time is 1928.

MAIN STREET FROM DIVISION. A loan office has sprung up in the Salisbury Times Building. Leeds and Twilley have their millinery shop in the next building, and there are now four drugstores in the first block of Main Street. The American grocery store is next to Read's on the corner. (Collection of Wicomico County Free Library.)

THE EASTERN SHORE TRUST CO. The Eastern Shore Trust Co. was born of the 1924 merger with the People's National Bank, founded in 1923. The sale of the site by Salisbury National in 1930 made it available and it was the Eastern Shore Trust Co. until its subsequent merger into the County Trust Co. of Maryland in 1932. It is now the offices of a number of local charitable enterprises.

FARMERS & MERCHANTS BANK. The bank's original name is still in the cement work on the building, but the bank merged into the Union Trust Co. in 1930. This company became the Signet Bank of Maryland in 1987. The building was sold to George, Miles & Buhr, an architectural/engineering firm, on November 1, 1990, and the building is used as the firm's home office. The Atlantic and Pacific Tea Co. was located on the south side, but their building has been occupied, for many years now, by Irvin Kamanitz's drug store.

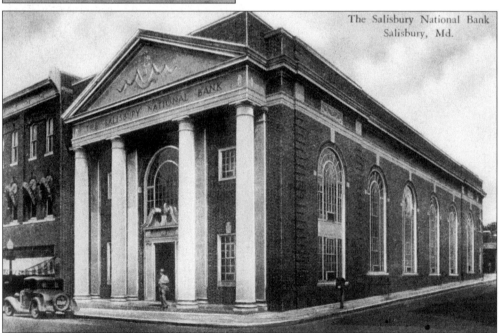

THE SALISBURY NATIONAL BANK. This bank moved from across the street in 1930, and built on the former site of the Peninsula Hotel, which burned in 1929. The Salisbury National Bank was merged into the First National Bank of Maryland and is still located on the plaza.

Main Street, Salisbury, Maryland

6258

MAIN STREET, SALISBURY. Parking is still allowed on the south side of Main Street. Bennett's Drug Store has taken over the corner store in the Building and Loan Building, and Read's Drug Store has taken over the opposite corner. John Kuhn Jewelry is in the next building on the north side. Bennett's store opened at this site in 1936, and Read's came to Salisbury in 1932.

WEST MAIN STREET. The central view is of White & Leonard, the last one of the four pharmacies to stay in business, but, finally, it became a stationery and furniture store. Lad 'n Lassie, next to it, is a children's wear store. Looking west, we can see Hess's, R.E. Powell's, McCrory's, Benjamin's, and Goodman's.

THURSTON STUDIO. The time is the Christmas season. The canopy in front of Kuhn's has been removed, as have the benches. Hess Juniors is in the store on the right with Johnson's Men's Store next to it. Beyond it are Mike Hal's and Edythe's. The picture was taken before the Fred Adkins Memorial Shaft was erected on the plaza and placed approximately where the Christmas tree is shown in this picture. The plaza was created in 1970.

Ten

HOSPITAL CARE

The Peninsula General Hospital, containing six beds and located in a house on Fitzwater Street, was founded in 1897 by Dr. George W. Todd. It moved to its present location at South Division and Locust Street in 1904. It was the first general hospital outside of Baltimore. Its School of Nursing was started in 1905, and a separate building was built for nurses in 1908. It celebrated its 100th anniversary in 1997; during that time its land space has increased sixfold, its square footage of building has multiplied by nearly 100, and its staff of doctors, nurses, and other personnel has grown beyond measure. Dr. Todd resigned as the superintendent of Peninsula General in 1909 and founded the Pine Bluff Sanitarium, which operated as a private sanitarium until 1925, when it was taken over by the state. A two-story brick building was then added. The state finally closed the sanitarium, and the site was turned over to the county to operate. It is now used as the Medical Access to Care Center. The Deer's Head Hospital, which opened in 1950, has always been a state-operated chronic disease hospital. Located on the northern edge of Salisbury, it has its own separate facilities, staff, and volunteers.

THE PENINSULA HOSPITAL. The building, when it opened in 1904, had a frontage of 38 feet and two wings, each 38 feet long. The hospital had a basement which contained a chapel, an embalming room, an autopsy room, a morgue, the staff dining room, and a kitchen. Electricity and water came from the Jackson Brothers's mill nearby, furnished without charge.

The Peninsula General Hospital and Nurses' Home. The new home for nurses was built in 1908. A four-story building with a basement, it was 34 by 12 and was expected to cost $10,000. A fire escape has been added to the hospital. It was required for the safety of the patients and staff.

Peninsula General Hospital, Salisbury, Maryland

THE PENINSULA GENERAL HOSPITAL. This shows the new exit from the hospital, installed when the hospital required a discharged patient to be delivered to his car by wheel chair; it also gave the patient a protected place to wait if his ride was late.

THE PENINSULA GENERAL HOSPITAL. This shows the hospital after the new north wing was added in 1940. The wing was designed to hold 133 beds, but, when it was completed, it contained 175. It also contained new service quarters, operating rooms, and accident rooms.

THE HOSPITAL. This picture shows the hospital when its bed capacity was 400 and required a staff of 90. A new front had been added to the hospital. (Collection of E. Pusey.)

THE PENINSULA GENERAL HOSPITAL AND SCHOOL OF NURSING. This aerial view of the hospital shows not only the hospital proper but also the auxiliary buildings, the nursing school, the Watson public health building, the boiler plant, and two administrative and technology buildings. Division Street was still open, and the new hospital had not yet been built.

THE PENINSULA REGIONAL MEDICAL CENTER. The new hospital is shown here. A portion of Division Street has been closed. Carroll Street is shown on the upper right and Salisbury Boulevard at the bottom. The helicopter pad on the roof is also visible.

THE PINE BLUFF SANITARIUM. This picture shows the first building as it was in 1909. The support services were located in the center building, and the two wings with windows were for patients. One wing was for males, the other for females.

PINE BLUFF LILY POND AND HOSPITAL. This picture shows the sanitarium after the state took it over in 1925, and the new building had been built. It is much more placid than it looks today as the MAC Center.

DEER'S HEAD HOSPITAL. Deer's Head Hospital was opened on July 1, 1950. It was built to accommodate 284 patients. It is a chronic disease hospital and performs a function not available at general hospitals or nursing homes. The hospital has a very active volunteer organization who do much to relieve the needs of and entertain the patients. (Collection of Gene Wharton.)

Eleven

EDUCATION

Schooling for boys began in Salisbury in 1818 and for girls in about 1823. Education in Wicomico County hit a snag in 1867 when the county was formed, and all public school buildings in Wicomico remained the property of the counties from which Wicomico had been carved. Salisbury Academy offered to sell its building to the county for a high school, but the offer was rejected. Eventually, Wicomico emerged with a high school on North Division Street, an elementary school next to it, and other schools in various locations. This was the case until 1904, when a Baltimore architect was hired, a lot on Upton Street overlooking Humphreys's Lake was purchased, and money to build a new high school set aside. The following year, the contract to build a new high school was let. The cost was to be $15,650, not including heating and ventilating, and it was to be finished by August 1, 1906. In those days, there were two girls for every boy who went to high school because farmers and mechanics did not require a high school education. By 1908, however, a commercial course was added, and a building was rented to accommodate it. By 1913, more and more boys were going to high school, and enrollment was going up by 50% each year. The addition of high schools in other communities slowed the pressure on the one in Salisbury, but the increasing number of courses led to the demand for a totally new high school. A new one was built in 1931, but, by the time it was finished, the building was already too small. Two hundred students had to remain at Upton Street until a new wing could be added. The high school was outgrown again, and a new high school was built in 1954, the old one being converted into a junior high. Since then, two more high schools have been built, and one of them has been enlarged. Mardela High School is the only high school left outside of Salisbury. However, a joint deal has been arranged in Delmar—the high school is in Delaware, the elementary school is in Maryland, and the Delmar students go to both.

The Maryland State Normal School at Salisbury opened on a 20-acre campus in 1925 for the training of teachers in the public schools. It was Salisbury's first institution of higher education. On Armistice Day, in 1925, the Masons presented the Normal School with a flag pole in memory of their members who had fought in World War I, and pictures were taken of the event. New sections of the building were added in 1928 and 1932, and the enlarged building is now Holloway Hall. Then, in 1935, the state legislature changed all three normal schools into state teachers colleges, lengthened the course of instruction to four years, and made the first two years the equivalent of the freshman and sophomore years at any college in Maryland. At this point, a number of students began their college work here with plans to finish their college educations elsewhere. The college continued to grow; buildings and facilities were added. Finally the word "teachers" was dropped from the school's name, and a full college education in fields other than education were offered. At last, the name was changed to "university." Credit for much of Salisbury State University's development is attributed to Dr. Bellavance, the university's president until his recent death. The university now claims approximately 6,500 students, a number of colleges, and a research center. Buildings have been added, both onto the original campus and onto additions that have already been made.

Wicomico High School, Salisbury, Md.

WICOMICO HIGH SCHOOL. This is the original 1904 building. The lavatories, lab room, manual training room, and boiler room are all in the basement. On the first floor are two corridors and a classroom on each corner. The second floor contains two recitation rooms and an assembly hall. The principal's office also served as the school's library.

THE HIGH SCHOOL. This picture shows the building as it appeared after remodeling. The entrance had been dressed up and a new wing added, joined to the original building by a recessed corridor.

WICOMICO HIGH SCHOOL, SALISBURY, MD.

WICOMICO HIGH. This is a picture of the building, built in 1931, at its new location between East Main Street and Route 50, following the addition of a new wing. It has now been converted into a junior high school.

WICOMICO SENIOR HIGH SCHOOL. This is the campus-type high school. It was originally built as a series of separate buildings. Later, these buildings were connected by closed-in walkways. The school was completed in 1954, but it has been added to since.

THE CAMDEN PRIMARY SCHOOL. This school backed up to what is now Carroll Street, and only a few people, now in their late 70s or 80s, can remember being students there. James M. Bennett, later superintendent of schools, was, at one time, its principal. When a student needed to be disciplined, he or she was sent to the river bank to cut a switch, which was then used on their open palm.

EASTERN SHORE COLLEGE. This building was originally a church. When the parishioners built a new church, it was rented by the school board to house the new commercial course at the high school. Later, it became a business school; this picture and the next are from that time, 1910.

98

A CLASSROOM OF EASTERN SHORE COLLEGE. You can see here the necessity for an advanced business education that includes bookkeeping and accounting. But, in those days, you didn't have to study taxation. (Collection of Jessica Anderson.)

THE MARYLAND STATE NORMAL SCHOOL. This card might not have been made were it not for the flag pole donated by the Masons. The north wing, which housed the entire school when it opened in 1925, is shown here.

THE NORMAL SCHOOL AT SALISBURY. This picture shows the campus of the elementary school, which many Salisbury students attended. The normal school building and the elementary buildings are at right angles, and the narrow end of the college building faces onto Camden Avenue.

THE MARYLAND STATE NORMAL SCHOOL. In this picture, the second section of Holloway Hall has been built and joined to the first section. This second section was completed in 1928 and more than doubled the size of the structure.

MARYLAND STATE NORMAL SCHOOL, SALISBURY, MD.

THE MARYLAND STATE NORMAL SCHOOL. The third section has been added, and Holloway Hall is now complete. This third building was added in 1932. The awnings on the administrative offices to the right of the front columns indicate a lack of air conditioning.

THE SOCIAL ROOM, SALISBURY STATE COLLEGE. This picture shows an interior scene at the college. This was the Social Room, completed in 1932. It was the site of numerous campus functions.

THE STATE TEACHERS COLLEGE. This drawing by John Moll is from the second phase of the school's history after it had become a college. This was still the principal building at that time.

THE HOLLOWAY HALL AUDITORIUM. This building was completed in 1929 and seats 776 people. It was redecorated in 1982. Many events that are open to the public are held here, so the auditorium has become an auxiliary place of entertainment for Salisbury residents.

THE CAMPUS QUAD. The Quad received a face lift in 1983. The dormitories shown here, clockwise from left, are Nanticoke Hall, Manokin Hall, Wicomico Hall, and Pocomoke Hall. This picture was taken from atop Choptank Hall, a high-rise dormitory.

SALISBURY STATE UNIVERSITY

SALISBURY STATE UNIVERSITY—AERIAL. This aerial shot of the educational campus shows Holloway Hall in the upper-left-hand corner and the Guerrieri University Center in the lower right. It does not show the new Commons building, built in 1997 and now located at lower left.

THE ATHLETIC COMPLEX. The athletic complex is located on the easterly side of U.S. Route 13, but the State Roads Commission has built a pedestrian tunnel under the highway to give students easier access to the complex. The main campus is at the top of the picture.

Twelve
TRANSPORTATION

The original site of Salisbury was very small. Initially, the curving river route was preferred over the ditches, swamps, and sand pits that passed for roads. But the roads were improved, and coach, carriage, and cart became an acceptable means of travel to reach Salisbury. Railroads were the gift of the 19th century. Paved roads and air travel were bestowed by the 20th. Now, as the 21st century nears, we use them all—land, water, and air. Passenger service is now only available by air and road, but Salisbury has the second-busiest port in Maryland, receiving oil, gravel, stone, and similar products, and is a constant destination for loaded freight cars.

TRAIN CROSSING TRESTLE BRIDGE. The trestle bridge was on the B.C. & A. line. This line was organized in 1894 and ran from Claiborne to Salisbury until 1928, when foreclosure proceedings were instituted.

THE B.C. & A. STEAMER VIRGINIA. *Virginia* was built in 1903 and served Salisbury until 1924, when she was assigned to Crisfield. Water transportation via the Wicomico River Line ceased in 1928. The *Virginia* came to Salisbury from Baltimore on three days out of each week. Freight service by the Victor Lynn line continued until 1954. (Collection of Gene Wharton.)

THE UNION STATION. The Union Station, serving both the Pennsylvania and the B.C. & A. lines, was built in 1914 and remained in service until passenger service was discontinued. After that, the station was sold to a sign company.

★ RED STAR MOTOR COACHES, Inc.
SALISBURY, MARYLAND

RED STAR MOTOR COACHES. The name originated in 1926 or 1927 as the result of a choose-a-name contest. The company was then operated by Day & Zimmerman, a holding company of Philadelphia, until it went into receivership in 1927 and a local group bought it. They operated it until 1952, when it was sold to Carolina Trailways. The bus shown here was a 27-passenger bus that was used during the Day & Zimmerman period.

CHESAPEAKE AIRWAYS. Service to Baltimore began on April 5, 1946. The service continued until 1949; it was discontinued because no permanent post office subsidy was secured.

Today air service is provided by Alleghany Commuter, a division of USAir, and a second airline is being sought to serve the area.

Thirteen
FOOD, FUN, AND FROLIC

The tavern is an ancient institution; it combined the serving of food and drink with entertainment. All of the places within this category offered one or more of these items. Some are still catering to the needs in Salisbury, but most have passed by the wayside. Some may be clear in your memory, others may be remembered for something else, but they all offered, at one time, either food, fun, or entertainment.

JOHNNY'S AND SAMMY'S RESTAURANT. This restaurant was started by Johnny Testa and Sammy Cerniglia in 1946. It met with immediate success and, in 1950, a new addition, the Mid-Ocean Room, was added.

BILLS SEAFOOD INN. This was, for many years, one of the best restaurants in the area. Ethel, Bill Ahtes's wife, was known for her careful and competent management of the kitchen. When they built a place in Ocean City, they turned the original over to Bill Jr., who finally sold it to Robert Hastings.

THE MID-OCEAN ROOM. This room served the Rotary, Lions, Jaycees, and others, so it was always humming. On July 1, 1953, a corporation was formed to conduct the business of the restaurant and to provide a profit sharing plan for its employees. It operated until both former partners died. The Mid-Ocean Room became the Alpine Room, a place for fine dining. The Alpine Room was in the front with a separate bar in the back. After the original partners died, it gradually lost its luster. Several people owned and operated the restaurant under new names until it was finally closed. Currently, it is unoccupied, but still holds many fond memories for Salisburians who remember patronizing the establishment in its days of glory. It now faces demolition. (Collection of Gene Wharton.)

THOMPSON'S RESTAURANT. Thompson's was, first, a diner downtown. It was sold to English. Then Thompson's moved out to North Salisbury Boulevard and built the building shown here. Thompson sold this property to Frank Parsons. Next, it was the home of the Town Club and, after that closed, the property was sold to Danzalea, a retail garden and Christmas shop. It finally caught fire and burned down.

JACK'S SEAFOOD INN. Jack was one of the subsequent owners of Bill's Seafood Inn. He operated it successfully for a while but finally sold it to people who operated it as the Shanty. It was later purchased by the Country House store and torn down to build a new warehouse for its merchandise. A tea room is now being erected on the site.

THE SHELTON DRIVE-IN. The Shelton Drive-In was started by Christian Shelton and his wife. The business continued until 1959, when he died. The building has since been torn down.

AYERS DINER. Ayers Diner was a successful diner, a surprise because the owners had no previous restaurant experience. They opened it in 1957 on North Salisbury Boulevard and London Avenue. They sold it to Elmer Parsons in 1972. It is no longer in business. (Collection of the late Thomas Irvin.)

THE WORLD'S LARGEST FRYING PAN. This is a gimmick of the Delmarva Chicken Festival and is in use only at the festival. The frying pan holds 100 gallons of cooking oil and can cook 10,000 pieces of chicken a day. The festival was held in Salisbury the year this picture was made and was run by the Lions Club.

THE COUNTRY CLUB AND WATER SCENE. It was never a country club, and the water scene resulted from an iron standpipe in the pond shown in the picture. The Lakeland Club had a very short life. It was started by Howard Johnson, the owner of the Wicomico Garage, and was dedicated on November 2, 1940. Johnson was the commodore. The club lasted until the spring of 1942 and was a war casualty. Johnson then converted it into his residence.

NORTHWOOD BAR. This place acquired the reputation of being the "baddest" place in town. It was known by salesmen from New York to Richmond. It was the place where the sexes went to mingle. It was built in 1953 by Winfield Dennis, who operated it until his death. After Dennis died, it was operated, in part, as a place for women to go to see male strippers. It is now the home of the East Side Men's Club.

114

THE WILDFOWL CARVING & ART EXHIBIT. The exhibit lost its home when the Civic Center burned. They found a temporary substitute at the Carriage House on Winterplace Farm and put out this card to help publicize the event in its new location. The substitute venue did not interfere with the show; it was highly successful. (Collection of Silvia Taylor.)

THE WARD MUSEUM OF WILDFOWL ART. This museum has been built to house the expanded collection. Formerly housed at Salisbury State, the collection grew beyond the space available there and required a separate building. This building is at the east end of the city park. It is open daily, and attendance is a rewarding experience.

ARTHUR W. PERDUE STADIUM. After years of Class D baseball and years in which we had no professional ball at all, a partnership headed by Frank Perdue brought professional baseball back to Salisbury. It is now in its third year and, last year, attracted more than 200,000 fans to its games, passing in attendance cities like Charleston, South Carolina. They won the pennant in 1997. Dinner is available at all games, as you can see.

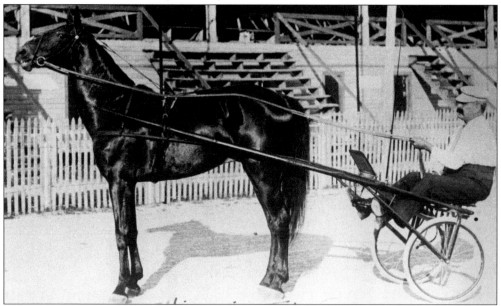

THE WICOMICO COUNTY FAIR. The Fair Association held its first fair August 17–20, 1909. A grandstand seating 3,500 people was built on top of a display building, containing agricultural products and homemakers' exhibits. As you can see from the card, harness horse-racing was one of the fair's staples and 160 horses were expected annually. The fair continued until 1933, when it ceased to operate because of the Depression. In May 1940, the Jaycees brought back harness racing to its Strawberry celebration, held at the fairgrounds. The buildings have been torn down, and an apartment complex built on the former fairground. It was at the corner of Parsons Road and Pemberton Drive. (Collection of the late Ruth Heam Parsons.)

Fourteen
MISCELLANY

This category is the clean-up one; it contains everything that does not fit anywhere else. There are pictures of some government buildings, homes for the aged, the radio station and newspaper buildings, factories, one retail store that was off the beaten track, a monument, a saloon, a black undertaker, and a Fourth of July meeting of the National Guard, all of which are important glimpses into our past history.

W.D. SMITH. This picture shows the tavern of Walborn D. Smith trading as Fountain House. It was located on East William Street near Railroad Avenue in the late 1880s and 1890s. It was a typical building of the period, a low structure built on brick pilings with a low front porch. The four wooden posts around the building are too short for hitching posts, but were probably for the protection of the building. Walborn Smith would have been put out of business by 1900, when this part of the county went dry. If that is Walborn in the doorway, he has at least three customers. (Collection of Dr. Laurence Claggett.)

Company I, First Maryland National Guard. The only person positively identified in this picture is the man in the middle with a sword—H. Winter Owens, the first lieutenant who was elected in 1905. The man on the horse may be Louis P. Coulbourne, the captain. The drill hall had been at the corner of East Church and William Streets, but it burned in 1906 and left the company homeless. (Collection of Robert P. Cannon.)

THE JACKSON ICE CO. This picture, dated July 1907, bears Fred A. Grier Jr.'s initials and identifies its subject as the Jackson Ice Co. plant. The only ice company on record in which a Jackson was an investor was the Maryland Ice Co., a Delaware corporation of which Sen. W.P. Jackson may have been president. It burned with a loss of $10,000 in July 1907. The manufacturing of ice began in Salisbury on April 6, 1901, with a storage room of 30 cubic feet. Pond ice, however, was still being cut and packed in an icehouse in Salisbury in January 1904. Ice companies were built near the railroad because getting ice to the railroad was more important to the economy than selling ice at retail to area households. (Collection of Janet Carter.)

THE HOME GAS CO. The Home Gas Co. put out this card in 1908. It was addressed to Laurel but was sent by rail. Its cancellation shows "Phila" and "RLES R.P.O.," probably Philadelphia to Cape Charles Railroad Post Office. In 1908, all mail except local went by rail and was handled on the postal car.

THE ELECTRIC LIGHT PLANT. This building was built in 1904 on the west side of Mill Street, and new water-powered turbines were installed to provide 300 horsepower. The plant was the first to provide power after midnight.

JACKSON'S MILL. This picture dates before 1912, when Jackson's Mill was running full blast. William H. Jackson was still living; he died in 1915. No one had any inkling of the hard times to come. This plant had become a single product plant, manufacturing the large dovetailed boxes that the carboys of gasoline were shipped in. The oil tanker had not yet been developed. Gasoline was shipped in the big glass carboys, each one encased in a dovetailed box. When the oil tanker was developed, the need for the boxes disappeared, and so did the business of the plant.

Jackson and Weisbach Co's. Shirt Factory,
Salisbury, Md.

THE JACKSON AND WEISBACK CO. SHIRT FACTORY. This building dates from the same period as the mill. The shirt factory was built to provide work for the wives, sisters, and sweethearts of the men who worked in the mill. It supposedly was "Uncle Billy's" answer to the workers' request for a raise at the mill. Rather than give it to them, William H. Jackson started the shirt factory to provide another paycheck for the family.

A VICTORY PARADE IN SALISBURY. This picture is of a parade in Salisbury in celebration of Woodrow Wilson's presidential election in 1912. It was the first Democratic victory since Grover Cleveland's second term, and the Democrats wanted to celebrate. They did so by holding a parade. Notice the tall hat on Uncle Sam in the first wagon. (Collection of Dr. Laurence Claggett.)

THE HOME FOR THE AGED. This building began as the residence of Dr. Naylor, was eventually purchased for the John B. Parsons Home as its second location, and was sold to the Baptists for their Home for the Aged. It is now the Hotel Esther, which is not a hotel but a group of apartments.

THE JOHN B. PARSONS HOME. This site once contained a residence, but, after the residence burned, it became the Firemen's Park. It was subsequently purchased by former-Governor Jackson, and he built a home for his daughter here. The central building is that home. It was purchased by the John B. Parsons Home, and the wings on either side of the central building became the residential wings. The city water standpipe can be seen in the background.

122

THE FUNERAL HOME AT 324 E. CHURCH. This card was put out by James F. Stewart, the only black funeral director in Salisbury. He went into business in 1919 and continued until his death in 1950. His funeral home was at 324 E. Church, where this picture was taken. The site is now in the street bed of U.S. 50. (Collection of Dr. Laurence Claggett.)

THE HUB UNDERSELLING STORE. This store was operated by a merchant whose customers were lower-income people, people who were very price-conscious. His store was in the Richardson Building located on East Church and Isabella. The building has a very distinctive pattern in its brick. The time was before World War II.

Parson's Cemetery, Division Street, Salisbury, Md.

PARSONS CEMETERY. This started as a private plot before the Civil War, but, when the Union soldiers were buried in the city cemetery, Parsons rapidly became the place to be buried, helped by the removal of the bodies from the Episcopal church when it acquired the cemetery. It has bought more land and a philanthropist has provided a brick wall.

THE PUSEY TYDOL STATION. This card shows the Pusey Tydol Station, which was at the time one mile north of Salisbury. It is now within the city limits. The other building shown was, then, the Town Club. In the 50-odd years that have elapsed since this picture was taken, this area has become almost totally Automobile Heaven. It is in the Maple Plains development of the Larmar Corporation. (Collection of James Jackson.)

THE WICOMICO FREE LIBRARY. This picture tells only half the tale. You can see that the flying buttresses were left when the building was converted from an armory to a library. The retaining wall that kept the armory secure from the drop-off on the adjoining lot also remained. In 1979, the library had outgrown its original 21,000 square feet and had to more than double its size to 50,000. It now has shelf space for 175,000 volumes. Arthur Goetz was the librarian who engineered the addition. The library presently occupies a full block between Circle Avenue and Market Street.

THE DAILY TIMES. This newspaper is the lineal descendant of the first daily newspaper of Salisbury, the *Salisbury Times*. It began publication on December 3, 1923, from 114 Main Street. The paper was sold to the Brush-Moore Newspapers of Canton, Ohio, in 1937, and, in 1967, it was resold to Thomson Newspaper, Ltd., of Toronto. It was then an evening paper, but in 1989 it became a morning paper. The paper bought the site of the old high school (which was also the site of a Union soldiers' camp during the Civil War), built the building shown here in 1957, and then became the *Daily Times*. Its circulation now covers the lower Maryland Shore; Sussex County, Delaware; and Accomack County, Virginia.

SALISBURY MOOSE LODGE NO. 654. The Moose Lodge was chartered in Salisbury on November 2, 1947. In 1952, the group bought 5 acres on the Snow Hill Road and built a lodge building. At least four additions have been added to the building shown here, and the members now say that the land, building, and furniture are worth in excess of one million dollars.

THE WAR MEMORIAL. Salisbury is not a monumental city; there are only three monuments. This one stands on North Salisbury Boulevard and is inscribed "In honor of all those from Wicomico County who lost their lives in the service of their country." This covers all wars and peacetime incidents.

THE NEW POST OFFICE. This post office was dedicated on February 18, 1967, a week late because of inclement weather. Franklin P. Coulbourne was postmaster. The post office building was unique, not only because it was located out of the downtown area, but also because it was built on a leased basis with a 35-year lease due to expire in 2002. It contained 45,500 square feet of space. At the present time, the lease has been terminated, and the property belongs to the government. It is currently due to be remodeled at a cost of approximately $700,000.

THE BLAIR L. CROCKETT ARMORY. This building was accepted by the state on October 23, 1958; it contains 31,171 square feet of space. It was rededicated to Blair Lee Crockett on February 20, 1982. Crockett enlisted in the National Guard at age 18 and served until June 1975, 41 years later. He served as a non-commissioned officer and a commissioned officer during this time. He received a battlefield commission in Normandy. Naming the armory after him was a well-deserved honor.

WBOC. The letters BOC stand for Between Ocean and Chesapeake. The AM Station opened on September 13, 1940. The FM station went on the air in 1948, and the TV station broadcast its first pictures on July 4, 1954. WBOC got an increase in power in 1962 and was sold, in 1965, to the *Baltimore Sun*, which operated the station until 1980, when the TV station and the radio stations were sold separately.

THE SALISBURY MALL. The Salisbury Mall was the first enclosed mall built in Salisbury. It was built in 1966 and was finally sold to the Equitable Life Insurance Co. When a new larger shopping mall was built north of Salisbury, some of Salisbury Mall's principal tenants, like Sears and the Hecht Co., did not renew their leases for space. The mall went downhill from there until it was tenanted almost entirely by antique shops. It has since been sold and is being remodeled.